INSPIRE YOUR CHILDREN

12 Practical Steps to Help Your Christian Child Succeed

Siau Smith

Published in Australia by
Bible Press
Address: PO Box 183 Forest Hill Vic 3131
Tel: 0487299206
Email: GSSbooklets@gmail.com
Website: www.inspireyourchildren.com.au

First published in Australia 2016
Copyright © Siau Smith 2016

All rights reserved. No part of this publication may be reproduced, stored in a retrieval system, or transmitted, in any form or by any means without the prior written permission of the publisher, nor be otherwise circulated in any form of binding or cover other than that in which it is published and without a similar condition being imposed on the subsequent purchaser.

National Library of Australia Cataloguing-in-Publication entry
Creator: Smith, Siau, author.
Title: Inspire your children : 12 practical steps to help your Christian child succeed / Siau Smith.
ISBN: 9780995397002 (paperback)
Subjects: Child rearing.
              Child rearing--Religious aspects--Christianity.
              Success in children.
              Parenting.

Cover design by Dalim
Book typesetting by Nelly Murariu, PixBeeDesign.com
Printed by Griffin Press

The Holy Bible New King James Version, Copyright ©1982 by Thomas Nelson, Inc. has been referred to throughout this text.

Disclaimer
All care has been taken in the preparation of the information herein, but no responsibility can be accepted by the publisher or author for any damages resulting from the misinterpretation of this work. All contact details given in this book were current at the time of publication, but are subject to change.

The advice given in this book is based on the experience of the individuals. Professionals should be consulted for individual problems. The author and publisher shall not be responsible for any person with regard to any loss or damage caused directly or indirectly by the information in this book.

Praise for Inspire Your Children

'In Inspire Your Children: 12 Practical Steps to Help Your Christian Child Succeed, Siau Smith reminds me of that same practical love and wisdom that surrounded me as a child. She does not outline a complicated set of instructions, but instead, provides tips that will give confidence to parents who strive to be the best they can be for the sake of their children.'

Mary Nelson, Founder of Mission Bible Class.
www.missionbibleclass.org

'I have known Siau Smith as a parent of children who attended the school where I am the principal so it is with some authority I can attest to her personal qualities, positive attitude, caring behaviour and the guiding principles she has always espoused in raising a happy and successful family. Siau has written this book from the heart, with the intention of sharing her experiences and knowledge of raising four children with other parents of young children. I commend this book to those on life's journey, as a practical guide to helping them establish the corner stone that will enable them to become responsible, well-adjusted and contributing young people in the future.'

Esther Wood
Esther Wood OAM
Principal Burwood Heights Primary School

'Some very interesting information and genuine reflection on child development. Your approach and information for the three major developments literacy, numeracy and social skills show great thought and knowledge. I have enjoyed your work. Well done and I wish you all the best with your book.'

Bronwyn Heller
Melbourne teacher – retired

'My reaction is from the perspective of someone who has no personal or professional experience in parenting. My overall reaction is very positive. The writing style is very accessible and readable. The approach is coherent and succinct. The use of Scripture is appropriate in the sense that the book lets the passages of Scripture speak rather than twisting Scripture to support a point you are making in the book.'

John P Wiegand
Attorney and Hymnbook Editor

'Siau Smith has inspired me to keep striving to pass onto our grown children the heavenly blessings, reminding of the power of the stories of the Bible that affect the future destiny of a person at any age. Siau inspires me to strive for a better learning environment, organised, planned and uncluttered and one that is comfortable with the right environment. Overall you have compiled many beautiful ideas that truly do inspire the reader, especially a spiritually minded reader. Thank you, Siau. God bless your efforts and love for inspiring parents' success in children.'

Elonie Cseszko
Relief teacher – Melbourne

*To my four beloved, wonderful sons:
Joseph Hartwig and Edward, Benjamin and
James Smith, my daughter-in-law,
Katherine Hartwig and my grandchildren
Chloe Hartwig and Jacob Hartwig.*

*They have brought blessings to me and
love, joy, peace, and trust in God.*

*Love you forever and like you
for the rest of my life,*

Mum Ma

Contents

Foreword 7
Introduction 8

Part 1

Chapter 1   Babies are born to read   11
Chapter 2   The power of words   19
Chapter 3   The sound of music   27

Part 2

Chapter 4   The importance of routines   36
Chapter 5   The importance of play   48
Chapter 6   A toddler's equipment   54
Chapter 7   A toddler's environment   59
Chapter 8   Spiritual development   65

Part 3

Chapter 9   Time to sit   74
Chapter 10   Conversations   81
Chapter 11   Meal times   90
Chapter 12   Rest   98

Conclusion 103
Acknowledgements 104
About the Author 105

Foreword

Siau is a wife, mother to four, childhood educator and committed and faithful Christian. In this book she shares her love of God, her immense gratitude for life, some of her own childhood and religious experiences; and her personal view and wisdom on parenting and childhood education. Raised in Kiribati, she now lives in Melbourne, Australia. Her book is a beautiful and inspiring story of love and compassion, written for the early years of parenting. In our fast paced and technology driven society, Siau's book brings humanity and goodness to the subject of parenting. It certainly made me reflect on my parenting approach. Siau offers ideas and suggestions that are accessible to all parents – love, time and care. If this book helps and supports you in any way, then Siau's mission to make a difference in the world will have been accomplished. I hope you enjoy reading her book as much as I did.

Tracy Busse
Waveform Consulting

Introduction

The purpose of this book is to give you easy, quality solutions that will help you teach literacy and numeracy to young children. The idea is to instil in children a love for learning that will last forever.

The Bible says, "There is nothing new under the sun" (Ecclesiastes 1:9 NKJV). In this book, I will explain how you can help children to develop their potential at home before they start school.

This book contains basic principles and skills for early childhood education and care. It is useful for parents, educators, and anyone working with babies, toddlers, and preschoolers.

I have always had a great interest in early childhood education and care. In the following pages I hope to promote love, respectful, trusting relationships, life skills, family values, and the importance of quality standards for all children and nationality.

I hope that the way I've written this information will inspire you.

Introduction

The book is divided into three parts:

Part 1 discusses my belief that babies are born receptive to the development of reading skills. When parents speak, babies hear.

In **Part 2**, I share routines that support toddlers' skills and development. A toddler's work is play. Equipment and resources are very important. A toddler's environment plays an important role in the safety, health, and wellbeing of the child and his/her family. Spiritual training is the most essential of all early childhood education, as God knows more about our development than anyone on earth. God created babies from the womb. I believe His Word, the Bible, is true, accurate, and full of wisdom.

In **Part 3**, I'll discuss how preschoolers learn educational activities while they sit peacefully, calmly and think for themselves. Preschoolers enjoy polite conversations and interactions with their family and friends. Parents, nurture your children by providing encouragement and praise. Nourish them with a well-balanced diet for growth and to protect them from illness. Meal times are special times for family and development. Everybody needs rest from work, especially children. A good rest with peace of mind makes them happy and wise. With your guidance, help, and direction, your children can be inspired to fulfil their God-given talent.

This book is valuable in content because of the wisdom of God. It will save you time and money from reading long books about parenting. It is easy to read, and straight to the point. If you have babies, you can read any of the three sections. Be inspired, and do the best you can to educate your children to be enthusiastic learners.

Chapter 1

Babies Are Born to Read

"And from childhood you have known the Holy Scriptures, which are able to make you wise for salvation through faith which is in Christ Jesus."
2 Timothy 3:15

"Blessed is he who reads and those who hear the words of this prophecy, and keep those things which are written in it, for the time is near."
Revelation 1:3

In the Bible, the Apostle Paul tells us that Timothy actually knew the Scriptures from childhood, most likely because his mother and grandmother taught him about their own faith (2 Timothy 1:5). Imagine the impact you can have on your children by giving them the gift of reading aloud and passing on your faith.

Chapter 1 - Babies Are Born to Read

Be patient and proactive

We all know that babies are helpless and cannot read by themselves, so someone such as Mum, Dad, a grandparent, or caregiver needs to read to the child. Reading takes time, love, and patience.

For children, time spent together translates as love. Children thrive on quantity and quality time with their parents and caregivers. You can help your babies as they learn to read by giving them some of your precious time. It's even more powerful for your babies to see you reading the Scriptures.

Reading times provide comfort for your children, increase their vocabulary and intelligence, improve their language development, teach them listening skills, develop life skills from the content of the story, foster a time of bonding, strengthen emotional security, and show them tender loving care.

The power of the spoken word

God created people with two ears and one mouth because listening is more important than speaking. Children who listen well will learn to read better and communicate more. Your baby can't understand, talk, or speak yet, so they need to listen and hear

Inspire Your Children

you as you talk and read to them. Children speak naturally because you talk to them, and they listen and hear the language constantly. It's the same with reading. The more you read to your babies and toddlers, the more they learn to read and be inspired to love reading.

Learning to read is a process. Reading aloud and telling stories promotes language development. Babies learn to recognize words, and that is the beginning of reading. We don't know how the brain works, but we do know that if you read to babies, they will grow to love reading and also develop their vocabulary.

Babies need language accompanied by a rich visual environment to enhance their language development.

Start early, and be consistent

Studies have found that at three months in the womb, your baby listens while you speak and sing songs. If you are pregnant, be careful what you say, because your baby is listening.

One news report on TV discouraged parents from reading to their babies. The news reporter expressed that parents who read to their babies may be trying to produce geniuses or are pushing education too early.

Babies can't read overnight, and the "baby media" industry shouldn't expect babies to read within a certain number of months or years. Children are unique and different, and each learns at his or her own pace. Don't be anxious if your child is not reading yet, but keep on reading to them, talking to them, and listening to them when they start to talk. Once they start reading, let them read the story aloud and congratulate their success to build their confidence and self-esteem.

You are responsible to help and support your children's learning. Don't wait until your child starts preschool; start reading to your babies, toddlers, and preschoolers today and everyday. This book will encourage your family to start reading, if you haven't started yet. It doesn't matter what the media may say to discourage parents about reading. The media industry doesn't care and is not responsible for educating your child. It is your God-given responsibility, not the TV's.

Establish a routine

When your infant is born, it's a very busy season as you try to establish baby's routine. After a few months, when your baby is awake and looking at things, it's a good time to start reading to your child. This is how children learn the language.

You should have a daily routine for reading to your baby. In Chapter 4, we will talk about a typical routine to help your child. For example, read in the morning, before lunch, after dinner, before bedtime. Whatever time suits you. Short sessions of reading are better than watching a half hour of television. When you read a bedtime story, it might be wise to select inspirational stories or books that relate to bedtime. Use the opportunity to build your child's faith as they listen to the stories.

After reading to your baby every day, repeating the same words for several months, you should notice your child's vocabulary developing. That is a sign that your baby is learning to read. Your child improves as you continue to read, as he or she listens to the words.

Explore resources

The library is free and a wonderful place to borrow books or participate in story times for children. Select quality books that are fun and good for babies, such as nursery rhymes or Dr Seuss' books.

Have patience when your baby asks you to read the same story repeatedly, and point to the word as you read. Repetition is the key to learning.

Be creative

There are many ways you can encourage your baby to read words. One way is to label items, point at the word, and say it.

Be creative and have different sound effects to make stories interesting. Reading a picture wordbook with a word and an illustration helps your baby to learn the name of items. For example, as you read, you could point to the picture and the word: "This is a flower. It's a pretty flower. That's the moon up in the sky."

Choose meaningful material

A family devotional time of evening reading instead of watching television will impact your children's learning habit and behaviour. They will forever remember these special times and cherish them even when they are grown up.

When I was growing up, my family read the Bible every night after dinner, sang a few hymns, and

Inspire Your Children

prayed. I believe this routine and continual exposure was instrumental in giving me a lifelong love for the Bible.

SUMMARY

- ★ Set a routine for reading times.
- ★ Let your children see you reading often and consistently.
- ★ Libraries, the internet, and bookstores have countless resources for children's books.
- ★ A child's favourite story should be read repeatedly with love and patience.
- ★ Help develop your children's listening skills by talking to them, reading to them, and listening to audio recordings.
- ★ Label items around the home to familiarize children with words.
- ★ Read many children's books per week to increase your child's vocabulary.
- ★ Include Bible stories to help your children grow wise and develop a strong faith in God.

Chapter 2

The Power of Words

"The first of all the commandments is: Hear, O Israel, the LORD our God, the LORD is One. And you shall love the LORD your God with all your heart, with all your soul, with all your mind, and with all your strength."
Mark 12:29-30

"And if anyone hears My words and does not believe, I do not judge him, for I did not come to judge the world but to save the world."
John 12:47

"Watch your thoughts. Thoughts become words. Words become deeds. Deeds become habits. Habits become character. Character become destiny."
Margaret Thatcher

To speak to your infant is to communicate and develop their language. The word "infant" is a Latin word which means, "without language."

Inspire Your Children

When you speak to your infant, you are teaching the language, sharing the language, communicating, and connecting thoughts and ideas in words. In a couple of years, your baby will learn to understand some meanings of the words and be able to speak the language. By the time they start school, they will be fluent in their spoken language. If they can't hear because of deafness, you can still communicate in Auslan or sign language. The more you speak to your baby, the better your baby will listen, observe, and speak. It is the same with reading. The more you read to your baby, the better your child will begin to read. That's how their brains develop, learn, and grow.

Talk to your baby about your daily routine and what you are doing at the time, using hand gestures and actions. The more you talk and use different words; the more they learn to speak and increase their vocabulary.

Communication is important for babies and children to learn the meaning of words. You can interact with your babies using simple sign language, happy facial expressions, hand gestures, and questions. Your baby will listen and respond to your smiles, facial expressions, and sounds of familiar voices. The names Daddy and Mummy will become familiar sounds and after a few months, baby will copy the sounds and probably say, 'Dada,' and 'Mama.'

Don't underestimate the power of positive words

When you speak encouraging words to your baby and children, you are speaking life, truth, and purpose into their hearts and minds. The Psalmist says, "by the word of the Lord the heavens were made" (Psalm 33:6). Words that you speak are powerful and can have consequences, so be careful what you say.

Strive to speak inspiring words and blessings to your children. Our words and tone of voice should be enjoyable, polite and friendly. Daily words of encouragement build up babies' happiness, faith, and confidence.

Tell your babies and children that they are loved, valued, appreciated, accepted, and approved for who they are as human beings, whether or not they do well at school. Your child's human worth doesn't depend on his or her talent, ability, or accomplishments. If your child is talented in something, appreciate the talent. Recognize that

Inspire Your Children

he or she has done a fine job. Even adults want to be recognized and appreciated for who they are and for their accomplishments. Whatever children do matters, so as parents we have to teach them how to work with their hands, be responsible and accountable for their actions, and be pleased with a fine job.

Babies and children should be praised, respected, and encouraged in their strengths and not criticized regarding their weaknesses. Sometimes we hear parents telling their children negative words, hoping they will learn from it, but children learn more effectively from positive encouragement.

For example, if a child can't sit still at church, the mother might say, "Why can't you sit still? You are this, or you are that." The child will only hear what was being said. Negative words are damaging to children. Imagine if an adult said the same thing to you. You and I would react poorly to negative words, but would be uplifted by positive, encouraging words.

Children are more sensitive in their emotions because they are still learning how to deal with issues of life. They will become exactly what you label them to be. Remember, your words hold tremendous power. When you label your child, you actually put an invisible identification in their hearts and minds which will remain and leave a mark.

The Bible says, "Therefore comfort each other and edify one another, just as you also are doing" (1 Thessalonians 5:11, NKJV). Build your children up with words of affirmation and encouragement.

The way we communicate thoughts, words, feelings, or information to our children should be sweet, direct, and specific so they can hear with their hearts and understand. Proverbs says, "Keep your heart with all diligence, for out of it spring the issues of life" (Proverbs 4:23, NKJV). The heart and the mind are the centre for thinking, understanding, and reasoning. Believers in Christ are taught to have "the mind of Christ" (1 Corinthians 2:16). When you talk to your children, you want to demonstrate proper behaviour by having the mind of Christ. They need to know what is right and wrong, and be rewarded for right behaviour.

Parents' words are powerful, so use your words to guide, direct, and encourage your children. Speak positive words, such as, "I love you. I'm so proud of you, just the way you are. I appreciate you. Be kind, generous, and patient to your brother or sister. Look

Inspire Your Children

to the right and to the left; hold Dad or Mum's hand before we cross the road. I would appreciate it if you could wash your hands before and after meals. Please cover your mouth when you cough or sneeze. Pray before meals, and say thank you for the lovely meals. Eat with your mouth closed. Don't reach over the table. Say, 'Please pass the bread and butter.'"

My husband has an Australian and Italian background, where table manners are very important. Sometimes when our children use their fingers to eat finger foods, he would remind them to use their knives and forks. That's an opportunity to train them to use proper table manners so that they will know what to do in formal occasions. It is also important to respect cultural diversity and behave appropriately and show respect to family values and beliefs so that everybody is happy.

I once knew a wise teacher who always complimented her students with positive words, such as *beautiful, awesome, smart,* and *hard working*. Children like to hear their parents compliment them in front of their siblings or friends. Positive words of encouragement about their actions and behaviour build your children up, give them love, acceptance, approval, self-esteem, and confidence.

One preacher said that praise represents a child's worth to what he or she does. Praise is usually reserved for God, for His awesome mighty power in creating the heavens and the earth, and for the miracles He performed. For human beings, encouragement is meant to praise their work, and to build solid confidence, competence, and a feeling of success. Even young children can feel successful in reading, writing, numeracy, and school readiness and reach their full potential with constant words of encouragement from Dad and Mum.

SUMMARY

★ Words that you speak are powerful and can have consequences, so be careful what you say.

★ Language is important to live, to understand, and function well in life.

★ The heart and the mind are the centre for thinking, understanding, and reasoning, therefore keep your heart with all diligence.

★ The way we communicate our thoughts, words, feelings, or information to our children should be sweet, direct, and specific so they can hear with their hearts and understand.

★ Your baby will listen and respond to your smiles, facial expressions, and sounds of familiar voices.

★ Whatever children do matters, so as parents we have to teach them how to work with their hands, be responsible and accountable for their actions, and be pleased with a fine job.

★ Children like to hear their parents compliment them in front of their siblings or friends.

★ Encouragement is meant to praise a person's work, and to build solid confidence, competence, and a feeling of success.

Chapter 3
The Sound of Music

"... I will sing with the spirit, and I will also sing with the understanding."

1 Corinthians 14:15

"... speaking to one another in psalms and hymns and spiritual songs, singing and making melody in your heart to the Lord."

Ephesians 5:19

Do you remember any sounds from when you were growing up? I'm very fortunate that my childhood was very happy. One of the things that I remember as a teenager living in Kiribati was watching the movie *The Sound of Music*. On the island there weren't any theatres, so movies were shown occasionally outside on Saturdays—but only if it wasn't raining and the film was appropriate for families. Less than a hundred people attended—

some brought mats or portable chairs, while others sat on the grass and concrete. It was Christmas holiday, and my family and I sat under the sky watching a movie projected onto a big screen. That was the only movie I ever attended with my family on the island. My parents were very strict, and because I was a girl, I wasn't allowed to go to movies unless they went along as well.

Learning through music

A memorable verse from the movie went as follows:

> *When you read, you begin with A, B, C*
> *When you sing, you begin with do, re, mi*

The Sound of Music was memorable because of how the children in the film learned the songs by repetition. The teacher was fun, intelligent, lively, and knew how to teach the children music. Words learned through music are often more memorable than those heard through regular talking. Communication is essential and necessary as part of life, but children remember words more quickly and for a longer duration if they hear the words in a song.

How many words do you remember when you sit in a lecture theatre listening to a speaker?

Chapter 3 - The Sound of Music

We can't remember everything the speaker said; that's why we write notes so that we can refer to them later. Sometimes we can't remember things. Listening to lecturers is good for adults, but not for children. Children have a limited attention span. Their brains can only retain a small portion of presented information at a time.

Music and early development

Studies have shown that babies in the womb can actually hear the mother's heartbeat. Listening to music begins in the womb. Babies in the womb have developed their amazing ears to listen, so after birth, their listening skills will improve as they grow. As you rock your baby to sleep, your baby loves the melody, harmony, and rhythm of your voice; the sound of music soothes and comforts your baby's heart and mind.

Music and cognitive development

Music is part of babies' emotional and cognitive development. To guide and support their development, begin by singing lullabies, then move on to rhymes, such as "Twinkle, Twinkle Little Star." When your baby is a few months old,

introduce new songs, such as "If You're Happy and You Know It, Clap Your Hands." The more songs your baby learns, the more words they learn, which is good for their vocabulary and language development. Singing is also great for the heart and mind.

Understanding your child's temperament, personality, strengths and interests helps you focus on directing their learning and increasing their attention spans. For example, if your baby or toddler likes to listen to stories, you should read more books. That requires time and patience, even if you have to read the same story a hundred times. If they enjoy listening to singing, then learn more songs. Children aren't critical about your voice when you sing; they just enjoy your enthusiasm and positive attitude. They are also delighted when they hear their own names in songs.

Babies and toddlers also learn the alphabet by singing the ABC's. Music is the language that children listen to and learn. The sound of music is necessary for children's language development, physical coordination and movement, listening skills, social skills, and emotional development and expression. Sing nursery rhymes anytime of the day when they are awake to increase their memory and teach them about the world through traditional songs.

Music and spiritual development

Babies and children like music and love to hear the sound of Mum and Dad's voice. Use the opportunity to select songs that will build and develop their character. For example, try the song, "The More We Read the Bible, the Happier We'll Be."

God created our hearts and minds to sing psalms of praises to worship God and have faith in Christ Jesus, with gladness and thanksgiving. Teaching your babies hymns and spiritual songs is like learning supernatural melody words from heaven that will soothe their souls. Babies' brains are developing and memories and music will enhance their cognitive, social, and emotional development.

The delight of music

Toddlers naturally delight in the sound of music. When they hear it, they dance and move their hands, arms, and legs, and wiggle about. Their faces light up in response to the music. Some toddlers sing to their toys, pretending to sing on stage in front of a big crowd. Singing fosters imagination, role modeling, and make believe. Toddlers and children will have fun with appropriate music, and act in tune to the rhythm. Words and songs that rhyme accompanied with clapping, raising hands, and stamping feet help babies and toddlers to connect meanings to words and increase their vocabularies and language development.

Developing musical talent

Babies, toddlers and preschoolers are developing their musical talent. Many parents train their babies to play piano. I'm all for professional music tutoring, but what I'm writing here is to help and support your child's quality time and learning. Children who play a musical toy are likely to develop their fine motor skills, which will help them with writing and focus on their task. With these musical learning resources, your children can make their own fun with the sound of music. As they grow into preteens, it's worth investing in a quality musical instrument to learn.

Preteens who learn to play a musical instrument learn reading, patience, thinking, collaboration, and communication with other musicians in an orchestra, hand-eye coordination, and social skills that require teamwork in school and with family. By learning an instrument, your child's cognitive brain development works more and increases in musical knowledge, creativity, sound health, and wellbeing.

Researchers have said that music is one of the seven spheres of intelligences that helps children to be smart and successful in school and in life.

Through music, children also develop the ability to perceive tone, rhythms, and melodies and develop their auditory skills and ability to play an instrument. I should add that each child is special and unique—if he or she can't play an instrument, that's fine. They might be blessed with another talent.

Conclusion

Studies have shown that music improves academic and language development in the brain, especially in babies and children who learn music early in their childhood. Recent studies show that children, who grew up and enjoyed music scored high in their IQ tests, have excellent social skills, and a self-confidence that makes them more resilient. Listening to inspirational hymns can also build your child's self confidence, self-esteem, and strength in the faith.

SUMMARY

★ Music brings family and friends together during social events, such as concerts or choir.

★ Music helps develop children's intelligence and accelerates academic results.

★ Music improves social skills, teamwork, and leadership.

★ Repetition is important for learning music and for other development.

★ Music teaches patience and develops baby's listening skills.

★ Music builds confidence in children.

★ Singing and listening to music creates harmony and peace, and releases stress.

★ Words in the songs enhance children's vocabularies and language, thus increasing imagination and creativity to help with their cognitive development.

Chapter 4
The Importance of Routines

"But his delight is in the law of the LORD and in His law he meditates day and night. He shall be like a tree planted by the rivers of water, that brings forth its fruit in its season, whose leaf also shall not wither; and whatever he does shall prosper."

Psalm 1:2-3

"But we will give ourselves continually to prayer and to the ministry of the word."

Acts 2:4

The environment must be carefully designed to protect your child's routines and to manage them safely and effectively. A toddler's daily routine involves developing life skills and encouraging good habits, such as getting dressed, washing their face, combing their hair, eating breakfast, and brushing teeth are good for their health and wellbeing. Explain to your children the reason why they do what they do. For example, a good breakfast makes them healthy and strong.

Tailoring your routine to your family's needs

Each family's routine differs because of the culture, environment, careers, beliefs, knowledge, skills, attitudes, and needs. For example, a family who lives in a cold climate will have a different routine from that of a family who lives in a tropical region. However, your child still needs to establish a routine to do tasks that are appropriate for their age, such as play, learn to read, write, and have quiet time. I know some families who have no routine for their toddlers. The children would have breakfast whenever, and after dinner, the toddlers would stay awake until the children were overtired. The importance of establishing a routine is partly for the child's safety, health and wellbeing, but also for learning and develop cognitive skills, good behaviour, and development.

Your family routine should be informal and flexible in comparison to formal schools, where every activity is on a timetable. In school, when the bell rings at a certain time, it means lunchtime or recess. It provides a sense of organization to a plan and establishes a structure, a routine, and a timetable to follow. Without a plan and a timetable, children are guessing what will happen next. Children like to know what their routines are, such as reading their favorite stories before bedtime. If they aren't reading before bedtime, they could be upset.

The family routine should be able to accommodate the needs of the rest of the family as needed. Your priority is to cater for the best interests of your own family. A baby's and toddler's routine is to make sure they are happy, feeling secure, comfortable, and able to adapt to their familiar environment.

Catering and altering routines

Most parents have a routine for each of their children. A baby's routine will be different from that of a toddler or a preschooler, because each has different capabilities and knowledge. For example, a toddler will listen to a story for a couple minutes due to short attention span, while the preschooler might read for longer. Reading is a very important routine, therefore, both Mum and Dad should have the opportunity to read and give a variety of voices to babies and toddlers.

Chapter 4 - The Importance of Routines

Structured routines are good for parents, toddlers, and children because they know what is expected of them and they learn to accomplish their chores and organise their time. Sometimes there will be a change in the routine because of work or a new baby, but the toddler will still be happy to have flexibility. However, reading a bedtime story is still important in their routine to help them settle down and to prevent overtiredness and stress. As they grow, they need adjustment to their routine to help and support their development.

Inspire Your Children

Baby's Routine

Graeme and Kristina Wall

I asked my friends Graeme Wall and Kristina Wall to share some reflections about what their baby's routine looks like from day to day. Here is what they have to say:

"I would love to say that I am super organised and we have a set number of activities and routines that we do each week, but unfortunately at this stage we are very flexible with how we spend our days. I struggle with this to some degree as I realize that children need structure and feel safe knowing what is coming next. It is always in the back of my mind that I need to sit down and make plans for us to maximise this time of development but most days I find that we do a combination of playing and going out.

If I were to put together a rough view of our day it would look like this:

8.00 – 9.00am	Wake up and have breakfast (our wake up time varies)
9.00 – 11.00am	Play at home or meet friends out or just go out for the morning.
11.00 – 12.30pm	Lunch

Chapter 4 - The Importance of Routines

12.30 - 2.00pm	One-year-old naps while the four years watches a video or plays with toys that the one-year-old can't have.
2.00pm - 5.00pm	Play or go out.
5.00pm - 6.30pm	Dinner
After dinner	Bath
	Depending on the time, either a bit more quiet play or straight into bed routine.
Bedtime routine	Stories Bible reading
	Songs
	Sleep time

We try to incorporate talking about God through the day, including singing Bible songs, watching Bible DVDs or reading Bible stories. We also talk about character and making good choices."

Chapter 4 - The Importance of Routines

Baby's Routine

Joseph and Katherine Hartwig

I asked my son Joseph Hartwig and daughter-in-law Katherine Hartwig to share some reflections about what their baby's routine looks like from day to day. Here is what they have to say:

"We are very lucky to have two fantastic children that we both love with all our heart. Our little girl was born in June, 2014 and our son in October, 2015 so with such a small gap between children, we feel that the discipline we had with their routine's made coping with the different challenges of life along the way much easier.

When our first child was born, it was naturally a very big adjustment for us. Katherine allowed her to demand feed for a little while, but the routine began as early as the second week of her life. We began with regimented feeds every three hours and pushed her to eat as much as she could within approximately a half hour period. We would wake her by changing her nappy most times to restimulate her to eat more. At first she would wake up before her set feed time and we often used a pacifier to keep her settled until it was the right time for her to eat. Despite this, it wasn't long until we needed to start waking her to feed.

I have heard some parents say, "I have never woken a sleeping baby." However, there are long-term benefits of waking them to eat at their set times. By doing so, your baby will learn to trust that he or she will always be fed, which will then allow you to begin to adjust their habits so they can start sleeping through the night.

By the time your baby is approximately six weeks old, their routine should be to feed at 7am, 11am, 3pm and 6pm, as well as a 'dream feed' (feeding your baby while they sleep) at 11pm.

I should say that getting to this point is not easy and requires a lot of sleep deprivation by the mother, but with the proper support from your partner, the short-term pain will allow you to have some normalcy in your life fairly quickly while keeping your child well fed and happy.

As you start to introduce solids into their diet (four months) and they start to consume more with each meal, you will find that you can start to bring the 'dream feed' forward each night until your baby sleeps from 7pm to 7am every night. There is no

Chapter 4 - The Importance of Routines

'normal' for when this occurs and every baby will have their own subtle differences that you will need to learn as parents.

The times mentioned above do not really change as they get older. At two years and three months, our girl mostly ate at the same time as her little brother, who was nine months old at the time. The fundamental difference between these two ages is that one was drinking bottles of milk before a meal, while our two-year-old ate strictly solids.

Some other things that helped us were regular, set nap times during the day. Your baby should nap three times a day until they're approximately six to seven months old, twice a day until they're approximately fourteen months old (some parents say that boys take a bit longer to drop their naps), and once a day until they're nearly three. If you can get your baby napping in different places during the day like the car, pusher, or shopping trolley, that can help your baby to learn to sleep in different environments. We are all creatures of habit and babies are no different. If you want your child to be flexible with where they sleep, you will need to teach them this flexibility from a very young age.

This is just our personal experience that worked with both our kids. Not all of this may work for you.

Inspire Your Children

You may need to adjust some parts of it to suit your work or other commitments. The underlying message I think is that from the time your baby is born, you will need to teach him or her everything, even things like the difference between day and night. If you need to get your child to day care every day by 7am, then you will need to adjust your child's routine accordingly. I find that it's not so much these specific times that keep our kids happy and settled, it's more the security they have from knowing that Mum and/or Dad will feed them, wash them, and put them to bed in a similar way every day and night and that's where their true comfort comes from. For those who are embarking on their journey into parenthood, I wish you all the very best. It's true what they say in that there is nothing that can properly describe the joy of being a parent ... you need to experience it for yourself."

Chapter 4 - The Importance of Routines

SUMMARY

★ Children thrive on routine for safety, health, and wellbeing.

★ Daily activities such as meals, reading, and writing develop life skills to prepare them for school.

★ Toddlers feel cared for, happy, and confident when they know that their routine is stable and consistent with Mum and Dad helping and supporting their development.

★ A toddler's daily routine is meant to develop life skills and encourage good habits and a sense of organization.

★ A toddler's family routine should be informal and flexible in comparison to formal schools, where every activity is on a timetable.

Chapter 5

The Importance of Play

"For bodily exercise profits a little, but godliness is profitable for all things, having promise of the life ... "

1 Timothy 4:8

"And also if anyone competes in athletics, he is not crowned unless he competes according to the rules.

2 Timothy 2:5

Play is the work, education, and achievement of early childhood. Toddlers who learn literacy and numeracy through play will be much happier and find learning easier and more enjoyable. This accelerates their progress. Naturally, children are very happy when they play their own age appropriate games. Toddlers are growing up and

Chapter 5 - The Importance of Play

they need a safe environment to develop their physical bodies by walking, running, skipping, climbing, and building.

Four types of play

There are four types of play activities that babies, toddlers, and children incorporate in their play: sensory, physical, cognitive, and spiritual. Sensory involves the use of their senses—for example: observing, listening, playing with sand, finger painting, felt boards, and play dough. Physical development has to do with their fine motor and larger muscles—for example: running, swinging, and hand eye coordination. Finger movement is good for developing their fine muscles, which will be useful for later writing skills. Cognitive involves brain development, their thinking and problem solving skills. Spiritual development involves the heart, soul, and mind, especially children singing, praying, and modelling Bible characters.

The importance of outdoor play

Toddlers and children should have time to play in the yard, and to be allowed to choose their own spontaneous play. Playing outside in the yard releases their energy by allowing them to

Inspire Your Children

run around and get fresh air, which are both good for their wellbeing and growth. They learn about themselves and the world in which they live.

Toddlers and children should be taught to be aware of certain health and safety rules. They can learn that inside the house is for walking, sitting, resting, reading, and learning. Outside in the yard is for running and playing. Children should learn to respect their area for reading and quiet time.

Creating an engaging environment

Toddlers should have a rich play environment with structured resources and unstructured play equipment to help and support their physical and cognitive development. They need educational toys and a clean, safe place to play. Suggested play items include an interesting ball, a dish of water, floating plastic fish and toys, a funnel, plastic cups, a sieve, a kitchenette, and dolls. Children will use their own imagination and creativity when they play to build their confidence.

Playing with other children

Toddlers who play together develop their social skills to be a good friend, share toys, and learn

verbal and nonverbal skills. Toddlers and children who play on computer programs should do it in moderation. Play is important for social, emotional, physical, creative and cognitive development.

Play is a child's way of life

Some people say that play is a type of recreation, enjoyment, and relaxation after a routine. Toddlers' and children's play is their lifestyle. It's the way they live, work, and learn. When children first see a toy, they observe it, shake it, listen to it, and explore it. They question, "What is it? How does it work?" When they first see a tricycle, they want to know what they can do with it.

Toddlers are naturally happy to play, are curious, inquisitive, and eager to discover their world. Play time helps toddlers and children learn to be themselves, and to know that they are loved, supported, and encouraged in their learning.

Chapter 5 - The Importance of Play

SUMMARY

★ Children learn and play for fun. That is their way of life.

★ Children imitate their parents' activities in their play, such as pretend play with their dolls, kitchen utensils, and reading books.

★ Children learn to play together with other children in order to develop their social skills.

★ There are four types of play that children incorporate: sensory, cognitive, physical and spiritual.

★ Toddlers can use play to learn about health and safety in their own world.

Chapter 6

A Toddler's Equipment

"Stand therefore, having girded your waist with truth, having put on the breastplate of righteousness, having shod your feet with the preparation of the gospel of peace; above all, taking the shield of faith ... And take the helmet of salvation, and the sword of the Spirit, which is the word of God."

Ephesians 6:14-17

Toddlers' equipment should be affordable, educational, practical, good quality, and fun to play with. For example, building blocks, slides, swing sets, walking beams, et cetera. When considering investing in toddlers' equipment, think about how it will support their physical

Chapter 6 - A Toddler's Equipment

development and learning. Having a few types of equipment to play with are good for their physical development. Many parents use toy libraries to borrow toys, thus saving them the cost of expensive equipment.

When planning your toddler's equipment, games, and toys, the purpose is to support their learning, interests, strengths, productivity, and to improve their physical development. Play equipment can help toddlers' movement and balancing. When babies, toddlers, and children play, parents should provide vigilant supervision and make sure that equipment and toys are safe and age appropriate.

Observe how toddlers use the equipment, games, or toys for the first time. Everything should have its own place, neat and tidy for safety. Provide them with help, guidance, and support when needed to avoid accidents and to build their confidence. Most toddlers are happy to play with kitchen utensils, sock puppets, ribbons, wrapping paper, and homemade toys and games.

Select a few games and toys that your children like so that they are not overwhelmed with too many choices in front of them. Each week, you could rotate the toys, games and educational resources, so that they are interesting and add variety.

Inspire Your Children

Children and screen time

Television and computer games are equipment that toddlers and children use for learning, entertainment, and babysitting. Sometimes it is safe for toddlers to sit quietly watching an educational program on TV while Mum or Dad is busy cooking dinner. However, when children watch too much TV and spend too many hours playing computer games each day, it is not good for them mentally, emotionally, socially and physically. Some parents don't allow their little ones to watch TV at all because of the influence on the minds of their children. Proper decisions and choices should be made daily for the sake of your children, whether to have the TV on in the background or to encourage communication, playing with toys, or reading.

Chapter 6 - A Toddler's Equipment

SUMMARY

★ Equipment, games, and toys help children's physical, social, and cognitive development.

★ Equipment must be safe, clean, of good quality, and age appropriate. Supervision is essential to prevent accidents.

★ Babies and toddlers are happy to play with kitchen utensils such as plastic cups, saucepan lids, and eggcups.

★ TV and computer games should be in moderation.

★ Toy libraries are useful to save costs on expensive equipment.

★ Too many toys can be overwhelming for children. Select a few at a time and rotate them weekly.

Chapter 7

A Toddler's Environment

"According to the grace of God which was given to me, as a wise master builder I have laid the foundation, and another builds on it. But let each one take heed how he builds on it. For no other foundation can anyone lay than which is laid, which is Jesus Christ."

1 Corinthians 3:10-11

"Blessed be the God and Father of our Lord Jesus Christ, who has blessed us with every spiritual blessing in the heavenly places in Christ."

Ephesians 1:3

Teachers and educators believe that a child's environment is also a teacher in and of itself. This means that the place where children live and play contributes a great deal to their learning. To ensure the best education for your child, it is important to provide a safe, educational environment for your

Inspire Your Children

children to play, learn, and develop their sensory, physical, cognitive, and spiritual skills to reach their full potential.

By providing the proper care and a happy environment, your children will naturally grow in confidence, and become successful in their own little world. When a person is content in their environment, they work smarter and more productively.

Three major factors affect children's growth and development: heredity, environment, and the loving care provided in their routine.

Aesthetics and designated spaces

The way you set up your environment depends on the amount of space available. Some people believe that certain colors on the wall can affect a child's mood, and hopefully help them relax and feel happy within the environment. Make sure the temperature in the room is comfortable, so that it doesn't hinder the children's creativity or productivity. A soft cushion for reading and listening to children's music will enhance the comfort level.

Chapter 7 - A Toddler's Environment

The equipment in your child's environment should have its own place. Children should know where everything belongs when it is time to tidy up. "A place for everything, and everything in its place." You could designate certain areas, such as a corner for literacy and numeracy, another area for art, and another for building with construction toys.

Children need a clean, safe, uncluttered, peaceful environment plus educational equipment to support their learning and concentration. The environment should have adequate learning resources such as books, art supplies, musical instruments, and science materials to cater for your child's learning ability and skills. Each child is unique and learns at his or her own pace. Children should be allowed to learn, observe, and discover for themselves what is real or pretend play.

Health and safety

The environment should also promote health and safety to protect children emotionally, physically, and morally. A child's dignity, privacy, and personality should be respected. Parents should do all that they can to ensure that their children are cared for in a loving and nurturing environment. This is a divine responsibility for which the parents will be held accountable.

Inspire Your Children

Be aware that toddlers will get into everything: the electricity plug, the TV, whatever they can touch. When they do this, they may not be misbehaving intentionally—they need guidance and age-appropriate learning materials to direct their time and play wisely in a safe, nurturing, and interesting environment. The environment should promote children's love of learning, and foster the development of certain life skills, such as reading, writing, mathematics, communication, planting seeds, cleaning a table, or washing a handkerchief.

Conclusion

Whether the environment is planned with education in mind or not, children will create their own play through imagination.

The best learning environment should challenge children's development by encouraging their desires, interests, and independence. A well-structured environment will cause children to observe and construct activities, and will promote questions, answers, and interactions with parents and other children in a healthy, encouraging way.

There are so many creative ideas to support children's learning environment. Provide the best learning environment that you possibly can.

SUMMARY

★ The environment contributes tremendously to children's learning and developmental growth.

★ Provide a healthy, safe, nurturing, and interesting environment to promote sensory, physical, cognitive, and spiritual development.

★ The environment must be clean and comfortable.

★ Three major factors affect children's growth and development: heredity, environment, and loving care provided by routine.

★ Each child is unique and special and learns at different pace. The environment should protect children emotionally, physically, and morally.

★ When guided properly, children behave well and strive for excellence in their environment.

Chapter 8

Spiritual Development

"This Book of the Law shall not depart from your mouth, but you shall meditate in it day and night, that you may observe to do according to all that is written in it. For then you will make your way prosperous, and then you will have good success."

Joshua 1:8

"But without faith it is impossible to please Him, for he who comes to God must believe that He is, and that He is a rewarder of those who diligently seek Him."

Hebrews 11:6

God has a purpose and plan for your life and for your children's lives. It is vital to pray and ask God for direction and guidance in this area. He has also provided His Word, the Bible, as our instruction book on how to grow and develop spiritually. We can read the Scriptures as if is God talking to directly to us, the same way He commanded the Israelites:

> *"And you shall love the LORD your God with all your heart, with all your soul, with all your mind, and with all your strength. This is the first commandment."*
>
> Mark 12:30

> *"These are written that you may believe that Jesus is the Christ, the Son of God, and that by believing you may have life in His name."*
>
> John 20:31

> *"Children, obey your parents in the Lord, for this is right. Honor your father and mother, which is the first commandment with promise, that it may be well with you and you may live long on the earth. And you fathers, do not provoke your children to wrath, but bring them up in the training and admonition of the Lord."*
>
> Ephesians 6:1-4

> *"And these words, which I command you today. shall be in your heart. You shall teach them diligently to your children, and shall talk of them when you sit in your house, when you walk by the way, and when you lie down."*
>
> Deuteronomy 6:6-7

Inspire Your Children

Infants depend on their parents and family for physical growth and development. In the same way, spiritual infants depend on their spiritual parents and family to help and support their spiritual growth, sustenance, and nourishment.

Spiritual development affects the human heart, soul, mind, and body. It is the most essential part of early childhood development, both for this lifetime and the life to come in heaven.

Religious instruction and spiritual development are not the same. Religious instructions relate to a set of laws, whereas spiritual development deals with the inner growth of the hearts and minds.

> *"The LORD said, I will put My laws into their hearts and in their minds I will write them."*
>
> Hebrews 10:16

> *"He who believes in Me, as the Scripture has said, out of his heart will flow rivers of living water."*
>
> John 7:38

> *"I rejoiced greatly that I have found some of your children walking in truth, as we received commandment from the Father."*
>
> 2 John 1:4

> *"I have no greater joy than to hear that my children walk in truth."*
>
> 3 John 1:4

Chapter 8 - Spiritual Development

"I declare to you the gospel which I preached to you, which also you received and in which you stand, by which you are saved, if you hold fast that word which I preached to you . . . For I delivered to you first of all that which I also received: that Christ died for our sins according to the Scriptures, and that He was buried, and that He rose again the third day according to the Scriptures."

1 Corinthians 15: 1-4

"For I am not ashamed of the gospel of Christ, for it is the power of God to salvation for everyone who believes, for the Jew first and also for the Greek."

Romans 1: 16

With parental authority there is also great responsibility from God. God expects parents to be obedient to God, and children to be obedient to their parents. We have to understand our divine roles and responsibilities to train our children and grandchildren in the Lord in order to have a loving, peaceful, and stable home environment.

There are similarities in the developmental stages of physical and spiritual growth. Physically, you encourage your babies and toddlers to learn to be independent, to do things for themselves. Sometimes we feel we are in a hurry to accomplish certain stages in childhood. For example, we want to rush our babies to sit, then stand, and walk independently.

But what about growing up in Christ and developing spiritual maturity? Are you in a hurry to grow spiritually? To grow spiritually, you have to be committed to the law of Christ, and to give up worldly things for the sake of doing God's will. This is hard work because it takes time and effort. For example, when you plant a seed, you need a good seed, fertile soil, water, and sunlight. God's Word is like a seed planted in your heart. That seed will grow if the heart is in the right condition, if it is watered with God's Word, and is in a good environment of the church where Jesus Christ is the sunlight.

Children are expected to increase in wisdom and knowledge. However, it takes time to grow—when you plant a seed, it will take time to grow and bear fruit.

As parents, it is our responsibility to bring up our children in the admonition and nurture of the Lord (Ephesians 6:4). What we do in our own spiritual development has more impact on children's spiritual development than on physical or cognitive development. Some people grow physically, but remain infants in Christ for the rest of their lives. Spiritual development is to grow from infancy to maturity in the heart and mind. The sign of spiritual maturity is when you are reproducing and bearing fruit for the kingdom of God.

Some practical suggestions for helping your children grow spiritually

Create spiritual memories about the Bible and the church while your children are young, and they will remember them and have healthy, happy, responsible lives. If possible, give your children the heavenly blessings by attending Sunday school. They will remember the Bible stories, which could affect their future destiny.

Find a church of Christ that is teaching the truths of the Bible and actively spreading the Word of God to the community to make disciples, to be trained, and to do ministry work throughout the world. This is the Great Commission that Jesus gave to His disciples before He went to heaven. It is the same commission to us today, because "Jesus Christ is the same, yesterday, today, and forever." Hebrews 13:8.

Inspire Your Children

My maternal grandfather and grandmother obeyed the Great Commission and went to do missionary work around Kiribati islands and Fiji islands. From what my mother told me, my maternal grandparents and each of their siblings were faithful missionaries in their mission fields. I believe that my family is truly blessed today because of the faithful seed that they planted for their future generations and descendants.

The only way to grow and develop spiritually is to read and study the Bible, join the true Church that Jesus Christ built, and unite with the family of God who are faithful to Jesus Christ and His Word.

> *"Train up a child in the way he should go, and when he is old he will not depart from it."*
>
> Proverbs 22:6

SUMMARY

★ Know God's Word, believe God's Word, and do what God says.

★ Trust God and apply biblical principles.

★ Spiritual development involves growing within the heart and mind to reach maturity, and bearing fruit for the Kingdom of God.

★ God's desire is that all of us would believe in Him, be built up spiritually by our spiritual brethren, and be supported, sustained, and nourished by His Word.

★ Spiritual growth takes time, effort, and hard work, but there are eternal blessings for obedience to God's Word.

★ Our relationships to God are based on love, trust, commitment, and applying Jesus Christ's message of salvation to our lives.

★ It is important for babies, toddlers, and preschoolers to grow and develop both physically and spiritually.

Chapter 9

Time to Sit

"And these words which I command you today shall be in your heart. You shall teach them diligently to your children, and shall talk of them when you sit in your house, when you walk by the way, when you lie down, and when you rise up."

Deuteronomy 6:6-7

"If then you were raised with Christ, seek those things which are above, where Christ is, sitting at the right hand of God."

Colossians 3:1

Sitting down is very important for preschoolers. They need to concentrate while they learn. Children must learn to sit after a structured routine. They can sit at a table or sit in a circle to listen to a story. Sitting in a circle for a short time is better when there are fewer children. This allows them to have a better view if the flip chart or activity board is in the centre. Circle time is good for social skills, as it can foster a feeling of togetherness and community through talking and asking questions.

Circle time is much easier for the leader because all the children are the audience, whereas teaching an individual requires more work and time for each. For example, if you have a flip chart for each child, telling the same story to each child is time consuming if there are many children. Circle time is easier for story time because everyone can listen at the same time. It's the learning process that is important.

Sitting down is a routine for children to learn best with a chair and table. Children who are trained to sit down at home are well-behaved anywhere, such as at church or at formal events. Their small table becomes their workstation. They learn math, language, label the names of the fruits, and do activities such as make sandwiches.

Preschoolers need a quality learning environment: a school that has rich, varied learning resources from practical skills, language, sensorial, math, art, and music, and also caters for different learning styles.

Learning while sitting down on the floor is also important to children when they do puzzles, build with coloured, wooden mega blocks, Legos, and pre-math skills.

Inspire Your Children

Sitting at the table provides opportunities to develop fine motor control. Pre-writing skills include playing with play dough, cutting it with a plastic scissors, moulding it into numbers, shapes, and sizes. Show them how to practice handling the plastic scissors by safely cutting the play dough. Children enjoy playing with play dough. They poke, pull, roll, flatten, pound, and thump the play dough. These activities strengthen their hands and fine muscles in their fingers as pre-writing skills.

After children master the scissors, they can cut circles, lines, zigzags, shapes and art paper.

Sitting down at the table helps them to concentrate while painting with large brushes or finger painting. They learn to make decisions, what colours to choose from, whether to use a brush, a sponge, shapes, or finger painting. Preschoolers are active learners and want to do their activities right and independently. Encourage the preschoolers' interests, strengths, and positive attitudes in their learning.

Preschoolers enjoy pretend play as part of early childhood development. They pretend to shop with plastic items, play with kitchenette and family dolls.

The home and kindgarten should have quality educational resources so that children play individually

and learn with real items, such as math cubes and science equipment. Every early childhood educational school is different and that is why parents have to find the best place for their preschooler. Your child needs a quality learning centre that is serious about the Bible, language, mathematics, science, arts, etc. In science, they learn about the weather and the universe; in math, they learn about trigonometric shapes, such as squares, triangles, rectangles, and solving math problems with real, wooden mathematical blocks. They handle quality educational materials with their hands because children learn in concrete and visual recognition of words in pictures.

At home, children have lots of time to pretend play with what is available and familiar. Most of the time, learning is not structured, and that makes sense. Children attend preschools to learn real life skills to reach their full potential, without wasting time on pretend play. You can give your children balance of learning instead of pretend play all day. Provide cushions for reading and a display of books on a shelf that is at the child's eye level to meet individual interests and encourage literacy. Children know how to turn the pages carefully and pretend to read by looking at picture books and stories.

You can read poetry, rhymes, and memorizing words and phrases to your children to build their vocabulary and language. Memorise the Golden Rule: "Do unto others what you want them to do unto you." There are many table and floor activities for preschoolers to help and support their brain, social and emotional development. For example, connecting Duplo blocks, drawing, colouring with crayons, playing with musical instruments, felt board, gluing arts, pegboard numbers and letters, etc.

Play Dough Recipe

1 cup flour
1 cup water
½ cup salt
1 tablespoon cream of tartar
1 tablespoon cooking oil
Food colouring
Mix water, salt, oil, cream of tartar, and food colouring in a saucepan and heat until warm. Add flour and put the dough onto a lightly floured board and knead until smooth.

SUMMARY

★ Quality early childhood schools provide a rich learning environment for children to develop cognitively and in all learning styles such as sensory, talking, asking questions, and modelling.

★ Sitting down is a skill that children need to learn from home so that they can concentrate to listen and communicate with family and friends.

★ Children can sit at the table, on the cushion, or in a circle on the floor and feel a sense of community.

★ Circle time makes listening and questioning easier.

★ Children learn more and concentrate better individually at the table.

★ They learn language, math, science, solving educational problems, writing, reading, and sensory, social, and emotional skills while sitting down.

Chapter 10

Conversations

"And the disciples came and said to Jesus, 'Why do You speak to them in parables? He answered and said to them, because it has been given to you to know the mysteries of the kingdom of heaven."

Matthew 13:10-11

"Rabbi, we know that You are a teacher come from God; for no one can do these signs that You do unless God is with him.' Jesus answered, 'Do not marvel that I said to you, 'You must be born again.'"

John 3:7

When we talk to our children, our conversation is informal. Children talk, we listen. We talk to children, they listen.

Communication builds trust, nurtures relationships, encourages the child's self-esteem, promotes good behaviour, and develops language and learning. Children are capable learners, and with the proper ways to communicate, you can bring out the best in your children.

Inspire Your Children

Here are some important tips for communicating with children:

- ★ Sit down or get down to the child's eye level
- ★ Speak face to face to your child
- ★ Do not yell or shout
- ★ Show respect and care by pronouncing the child's name correctly
- ★ Speak with a loving attitude and soft tone

Our conversations to children must be friendly and understanding. Preschoolers develop their language skills through communication, interaction, listening, and talking. Children communicate their needs, wants, emotions and feelings through conversations with their parents and other children. Sometimes children fight over a toy because they haven't learned how to share or converse politely. Children learn to talk because you talk to them, read to them, and model the right way to communicate ideas and information.

Teaching children to communicate politely with speech or sign language is important. It is part of fulfilling their aspirations as individuals, and getting along well as families, as students, and as communities.

Children can learn good manners through singing songs aloud, like these:

The Good Manners Song
Tune: This is the Way
Author unknown

This is the way we ask for something
We ask for something, we ask for something
This is the way we ask for something
Saying, Please and Thank you.
This is the way we play and be kind
We play and be kind
We play and be kind
This is the way we play and be kind
Sharing and being good friends.

The Please and Thank You Song
Tune: Frere Jacques
Author unknown

Please and Thank you
Please and Thank you
Sounds so nice
Sounds so nice
Manners are important
Manners are important
Be polite
Be polite

Chapter 10 - Conversations

Children love the sounds of repetition, rhyme, and rhythm. Teach good manners using the sounds of your words. Good manners include knowing in their heart what is right, saying what is right, and doing what is right. Children learn from their parents' beliefs, values and attitudes. They learn good manners through conversations and modeled right behaviour. Teach them how to share and be kind, honest, respected, trusted, helpful, caring and loving.

Children are naturally inquisitive and ask a lot of questions. As parents, it's important to answer each of their questions right away and not wait until later. The other day, I was listening to a preschooler talking to her parents. She asked questions and the answer she received was, "We're busy. Could you please ask the questions later?" The parents then gave her a mobile phone to play with. The preschooler was happy with the mobile phone, but I think she wanted some attention. Whatever we do, we should respond to our children's immediate questions and needs to show that we care.

Here's a scenario. If you are busy at work, for example, and your employer asks you a question, would you say, "I'm busy, ask me later. And by the way, here's my mobile phone to play with." Children have feelings and emotions, too, and they should be treated with love and respect, especially in communication. This shows we care about them and their desire to learn. Tell your children they bring you much joy even if they repeat the same question a hundred times. Communication improves their language development, self-confidence, and trust.

What do you communicate to your children? Tell your children that they bring you joy and blessings. It will shine a light in their hearts and bring smiles to their faces.

Children want to hear that they are loved, valued, accepted, approved, appreciated, trusted, important, and unique, and that you are proud of them.

Teaching children how to be polite and how to be good friends is important for their social skills, emotional development, and building relationships. They need to learn to be kind, show respect, and be courteous, the way they would like to be treated, even if others don't behave the way they should.

Preschoolers enjoy talking and interacting with other children, verbally and non-verbally using signs and gestures to demonstrate their feelings and ideas. The way we communicate is critical in any relationship, but especially in early childhood

Chapter 10 - Conversations

development so that children can grow, build trust and understanding, and be happy.

One of the best conversation habits you can have with your children is to talk without gossip, without the interruptions of TV or Facebook, and be grateful for the blessings you have.

Many years ago, people believed that children should be quiet when adults were talking, but studies have since suggested that children should be included in conversations, such as family time and meal times, to encourage their language development and interaction.

Communication with your babies, toddlers and preschoolers is great, but what is even better for them is communicating the Word of God, the true knowledge, because they will be strengthened in their hearts and satisfied and complete forever.

Communication to God in prayer and listening as God talks to us through His Word, the Bible, is wonderful communication. Through our belief in God and our conversation with God, we can help others and make a difference in the world.

I heard a story about a mother and her toddler who went shopping to purchase a new doll. As they observed the incredible varieties of dolls on the shelf, the toddler was allowed to choose a doll from a wide selection. The mother said, "Would you like this lovely doll?" The toddler replied with confidence, "She's wearing a bikini. It's not modest!"

The mother smiled and knew that her Bible class lessons had not have been instilled in her daughter's heart and mind. How else would a toddler understand what modesty looks like?

The Bible says that hearing God's Word can be hard because the heart might not be ready to hear. When God speaks from the Bible, we should be ready to hear it with undivided attention. The key to really listening to the gospel message is to use our heart and mind to hear God's Word.

SUMMARY

★ There are appropriate ways to communicate with children: sit down or get down to the child's eye level; speak face to face to your child; do not yell or shout; show respect and care by pronouncing child's name correctly; and speak with a loving attitude and soft tone.

★ Communication builds trust, nurtures relationships, encourages child's self-esteem and good behaviour, and develops their language and learning.

★ Our conversation to children should be friendly and relaxed, with appropriate body language, both verbally and non-verbally.

★ Children learn good manners through conversations and modeled right behaviour.

★ Preschoolers enjoy talking and interacting with other children, verbally and non-verbally using signs and gestures to demonstrate their feelings and ideas.

★ The way we communicate is critical in any relationship, but especially in early childhood development so that children can grow, build trust and understanding, and be happy.

Chapter 11

Meal Times

> "Jesus said, 'For the bread of God is He who comes from heaven and gives life to the world.'"
>
> John 6:33

> "Now may He who supplies seed to the sower, and bread for food, supply and multiply the seed you have sown and increase the fruits of your righteousness."
>
> 2 Corinthians 9:10

Meal times are very important times for children to enjoy a healthy and happy life. It is important to teach children correct eating habits that will last a lifetime. Children need to maintain a well-balanced diet from a variety of suitable foods. As parents, it is our responsibility to understand the nutritional values of food, such as vitamins and minerals, so that children are well-nourished and develop properly.

Chapter 11 - Meal Times

Water and exercise are also vital for maintaining good health.

Nutritionists place these nutrients into five main food groups: protein, carbohydrates, fats, vitamins, and minerals. Foods that contain proteins include milk, meat, eggs, fish, chicken, and dairy products. Grains, beans, nuts, and peas are also rich in protein. Protein is essential for growth, bodybuilding, and repair of body tissues. Children need foods rich in protein to grow and develop physically. They also need carbohydrates, vitamins, and minerals.

Carbohydrates are foods rich in starch and sugar, such as bread, breakfast cereals, pasta, and potatoes. Fibre can't be stored in the body but helps with the end products. Fatty foods are fats, butter, oil, and sugars. Fatty foods are present in most foods and should be eaten in moderation, as excessive fat intake can lead to high cholesterol. Vitamins are essential for good health and well-being. Carbohydrates and fats provide warmth and energy.

Vitamins can't be stored in the body, so it's important to have vitamins daily if possible. Foods rich in vitamins include oily fish, eggs, dairy products, vegetables, carrots, milk, fish, and fruits such as apples, lemons, and oranges. Vitamins and minerals are essential for the maintenance of good heath and for the fighting of infections. It is better to eat healthier, natural foods with lower calories that contain all the nutrients for a well-balanced diet and good health.

When I was in high school, I studied home economics and learned about food nutrients, values, and effects on the body, as well as the preparation of food to meet individual needs in order to maintain a well-balanced diet. For example, I learned how to prepare a meal for a child, an elderly person, an office worker, a hard-working builder, or a sick person. People eat differently according to their age, gender, occupation, climate, size, or for religious reasons. By understanding the nutrients, you would be able to cook a well-balanced diet to cater for the needs of your family.

We all need food to survive, and to be strong and healthy. Every culture has different kinds of food, and much depends on where they live, religious beliefs, money, and time. Some children are malnourished because they don't have enough to eat and don't have well-balanced diets. Some people have health problems because they eat too much without exercise. Some people have plenty of money and plenty of food, but eat unhealthy food, thus resulting in health problems. For example, too much fast food is unhealthy.

Then there are unsuitable foods for preschoolers such as sweet biscuits, cakes, chips, chocolate, cordial, and lollies. It's alright to eat these sweet foods, occasionally, perhaps for a birthday celebration or special holiday, but they should be consumed in moderation. The best foods to eat as snacks are good selections of healthy foods. It's all about changing our mindset and thinking about the right kind of food that is healthy and good for us.

We can make better choices to cook a well-balanced diet from the foods that are healthy and nutritious. Certain foods promote health and well-being, so it's important to understand the nutrients and make wholesome meals that babies, toddlers and preschoolers will enjoy. Meal times for toddlers and preschoolers are breakfast, morning tea, lunch, afternoon tea and dinner. Encourage your children to respect themselves and care for their needs, which includes eating healthy meals. Suitable foods for morning tea and afternoon tea for your preschoolers are cheese, cracker biscuits, dried fruit, fresh fruit, savoury sandwiches, yoghurt, etc.

It is important that children should have a small amount of protein everyday, along with other nutrients. A well-balanced diet is essential, but the preparation methods are also important. Meat must be properly cooked, and vegetables shouldn't be overcooked because of the vitamins in them. It's better to cook vegetables in a small amount of water to retain the nutrients and the colour of the vegetables.

Besides ensuring that your children are receiving wholesome nutrients to support their physical growth, meal times are also wonderful opportunities to build family relationship and invest in our children's character growth. Do your best to protect your family's time around the table. Develop strong habits and well-established routines around meal times so your children will look forward to the time spent together.

Meal times are also great windows of opportunity to instil spiritual truths and biblical principles in our children. Take the time to start meaningful conversations and ask poignant questions. After you finish eating, read a passage from the Bible and spend some time in family prayer. Meal times can be both physically and spiritually nourishing if you make the effort to plan ahead and develop healthy habits and strong routines.

SUMMARY

★ It is important to teach children the correct eating habits that will last a lifetime.

★ Meal times are very important times for children to enjoy a healthy and happy life.

★ Nutritionists place nutrients into five main food groups: protein, carbohydrates, fat, vitamins, and minerals.

★ Protein is essential for growth, bodybuilding and repair of body tissues. Carbohydrates and fats provide warmth and energy.

★ Vitamins and minerals are essential for maintenance of good heath and to fight infection.

★ It's better to eat natural foods that contain all the nutrients for a well-balanced diet and good health.

Chapter 12

Rest

"God blessed the seventh day and sanctified it, because in it He rested from all His work which God had created and made."

Genesis 2:3

"There remains therefore a rest for the people of God."

Hebrews 4:9

God created the world in six days and He rested on the Sabbath day, the seventh day. God didn't need a rest, but He showed a pattern for the Israelites and other people to follow. The Sabbath was created for people to rest and to sanctify it. Rest and sleep are necessary for body, mind, soul and spirit. God knows that people who continuously work for six days would be weary and tired and they need to rest.

It is similar with children. Children need to rest from their play. We have talked about play in the previous chapters. Play is children's work and they are most productive during the day because they are energetic. After a while, preschoolers get tired from their play. Preschoolers need to rest on a daily basis to promote health and well-being. The best time to rest is after lunch. Some preschoolers are so full of energy and hyperactive that rest is not in their vocabulary—but they still need rest. As parents, we know what is best for children and what they need.

Every child is unique and special and has individual needs at rest time. Most infants and toddlers need afternoon rest. Rest time is quiet time to sit or lie down and be calm in a peaceful environment. Rest is part of the children's routine. Don't wait until children are overtired. Children who are overtired may be likely to have accidents or misbehave. Children who are well rested tend to be more attentive and make better students.

Rest is important to children's emotional, physical, and spiritual condition. Children need to feel safe, comfortable, and stress-free. Play soft music as a cue so children know it's time to settle down. Develop a routine by playing the same, familiar song that is dedicated to rest time. For example, when I was growing up, every Sunday before worship, there was a hymn that we always sang before worship, which meant it was time to sit down and worship God.

The length of time preschoolers rest depends on the child, family, environment, and culture. At midday, rest time can be up to two hours in length. After children have rested, they can have afternoon tea before playing and running around in the yard to release their energy. Quiet time activities can include reading, writing, puzzles, threading, matching games, or play dough.

Rest times can also be helpful for parents, as the regular block of time each day can provide tired parents a chance to recharge their batteries or catch up on chores while the children are occupied.

Children may not like the idea of rest time, but well-established routines will benefit them in the long run. If you give them time to prepare in advance, they may be less likely to complain when quiet time arrives.

Chapter 12 - Rest

SUMMARY

★ The body, mind and spirit need rest and sleep for health and well-being.

★ God knows that people who continuously work for six days would be weary and tired and need to rest.

★ Preschoolers and other children need to rest on a daily basis to promote health and well-being.

★ Rest should be part of a child's routine. Don't wait until children are overtired.

★ Children who are overtired would be likely to have accidents and misbehave. Children who are well rested are likely to be more attentive and make better students.

Conclusion

I pray that this book will help you to make better-informed decisions to promote literacy, numeracy and spiritual education to your babies, toddlers and preschoolers. The more you understand your children's needs and the qualities God has blessed them with, the better and more confident you become as you nurture them and train them up to the best of your abilities. Continue to ask God for wisdom and direction, and use powerful words of encouragement to help your children reach their full potential. Enjoy your life and inspire your family with love, joy, peace, commitment and prayers as the foundation for success. Be inspired, and do the best you can to educate your children to be enthusiastic learners.

Acknowledgements

To God, my Heavenly Father, my Lord and Saviour Jesus Christ, who caused me to believe that with His help, writing this book was possible.

To my husband, Garry, who gives me encouragement and helped me persevere to complete this book.

To Julie Postance, author of **Breaking the Sound Barriers.** As my inspirational teacher and writing coach, she is the reason this book is completed.

To my children and grandchildren, who inspire and challenge me to be the mother and grandma that I am today. This is the reason this book is written.

To Heather Cox, for her encouragement and logo design.

To the ghostwriter and the editor Kate Motaung. Her honest literary style has blessed me in this writing journey.

To Paul Cox, for his artistic talents as an illustrator.

To the typesetter, proofreader and printer for their awesome work and putting the book together.

Thank You everyone for making this book possible.

About the Author

Siau Smith is a full time mother to her four sons and a part-time caregiver for her grandchildren. She taught in high schools in Kiribati prior to having children. She also worked in Australia as a qualified educator in numerous childcare centres. Her passion and interest is teaching the children the Bible, literacy and numeracy. Siau is also a Sunday school Bible teacher. She has written articles for the Kiribati Newstar newspaper, where she serves as one of the directors. In addition, Siau is a former Secretary and Vice President of the Melbourne Kiribati Group Incorporated. Siau and her husband Garry, live in Australia with their family and a pet turtle named Leo.